INVESTIGATIONS

IN NUMBER, DATA, AND SPACE®

STUDENT ACTIVITY BOOK

SAVVAS
LEARNING COMPANY

TERC

The Investigations curriculum was developed by TERC, Cambridge, MA.

TERC

This material is based on work supported by the National Science Foundation ("NSF") under Grant No. ESI-0095450. Any opinions, findings, and conclusions or recommendations expressed in this material are those of the author(s) and do not necessarily reflect the views of the National Science Foundation.

ISBN-13:   978-0-328-86027-2
ISBN-10:   0-328-86027-1

SAVVAS
LEARNING COMPANY

13 2022

UNIT 1 Counting People, Sorting Buttons

UNIT 2 Counting Quantities, Comparing Lengths

CONTENTS

UNIT 3 Make a Shape, Fill a Hexagon

UNIT 4 Collect, Count, and Measure

UNIT 7 How Many Noses? How Many Eyes?

CONTENTS

UNIT 8 Ten Frames and Teen Numbers

Counting People, Sorting Buttons

Counting People,
Sorting Buttons

About the Mathematics in this Unit

Dear Family,

Our class is starting the year with a mathematics unit called *Counting People, Sorting Buttons* from the *Investigations 3* Curriculum. This unit serves as an introduction to some of the mathematical routines students will do all year.

These routines include:

- Counting to take attendance
- Using the calendar to count days and to keep track of time and events
- Counting and recording the number of objects in a jar, and creating a set with the same number
- Counting and analyzing data about our class, such as how many students do (and do not) have a younger sibling

In addition, students are introduced to the manipulatives they will use in mathematics this year and to routines for using and taking care of such materials.

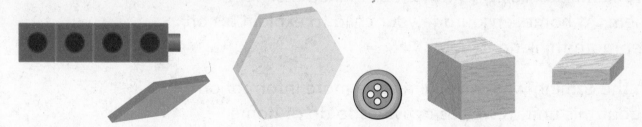

In this unit, students also use these materials to begin to work on sorting and counting. For example, they carefully examine a button and then look for attributes that some buttons have in common.

About the Mathematics in this Unit

Throughout this unit, students will be working toward these goals:

- Becoming familiar with the expectations for learning
- Exploring some of the materials they will be using to model mathematical situations and to solve mathematical problems
- Talking about mathematical problems and solutions
- Working with peers as they share ideas and materials
- Relying on their own thinking and learning from the thinking of others

In our math class, students engage in math problems and activities and discuss the underlying concepts. They are asked to share their reasoning and solutions. It is important that children solve math problems accurately in ways that make sense to them. At home, encourage your child to explain his or her math thinking to you.

In the coming weeks, you'll receive more information about this unit as well as activities to do at home.

NAME _____ DATE _____

Sorting Buttons

Circle the buttons that are round.
X the buttons that have 3 holes.

NOTE

Students sort buttons based on a particular attribute.
MWI **Sorting Buttons**

Related Activities to Try at Home

Dear Family,

The activities suggested below are related to the mathematics we are currently studying in school. Doing them together can enrich your child's mathematical learning.

Calendar Explore the calendar as a tool for keeping track of time and events by showing your child how you use it. When you write in an appointment or a family event, or when you use it to find how many more days until a special event, talk with your child about what you're doing.

Describing Encourage your child to describe the physical features of objects and to think about how objects are alike or different. For example:

- How would you describe this ball? (e.g., red, round, big)
- How is the ball the same as this box? (They are both red.)
- How are they different? (The ball is round, but the box is square, or the box is small.)

Also, encourage your child to use words to describe where a picture or object is in relation to another (e.g., next to, near, under, over, below, above).

Related Activities to Try at Home

Counting Take advantage of any opportunities to count with your child. Children learn to count accurately by having many opportunities to see and hear other people count and to count on their own. You can model this by:

- Counting out napkins or plates for the table
- Counting the number of stairs as you go up or down
- Counting the number of a particular object (e.g., dogs, signs, or cars) as you walk down the street
- Counting the number of items in a collection of plastic animals, cars, or other small toys

Sorting If you have a button (or other) collection, you and your child could talk about different ways to sort the buttons. Your child might like to teach you *Button Match-Up*. In this game, one player chooses a button, and then both players work together to find buttons that have one thing that is the same. For example, any button with two holes matches this button, as does any button that is black, small, or plastic.

Math and Literature You can find the following books in your local library and read them together.

Aber, Linda Williams. *Grandma's Button Box.*
Emberley, Rebecca. *My Numbers (Mis Numeros).*
Falwell, Cathryn. *Feast for 10.*
Gayzagian, Doris. *One White Wishing Stone:*
A Beach Day Counting Book.
Mariconda, Barbara. *Sort it Out!.*
Martin, Bill. *Chicka Chicka 1, 2, 3.*
Otoshi, Kathryn. *Zero.*
Roth, Susan L. *My Love for You All Year Round.*
Walsh, Ellen Stoll. *Mouse Count.*
Wormell, Christopher. *Teeth, Tails, and Tentacles.*

NAME   DATE

Describing Objects at Home

Choose two objects. Draw a picture of each object. Make a list of words that describe each object.

My object is a: _____.	My object is a: _____.

These words describe my objects:

_____   _____

_____   _____

_____   _____

_____   _____

NOTE

Students describe attributes of objects. Please help your child record the name and a list of words that describe each object.

MWI **Geometry and Shapes in the World**

NAME _____ DATE _____

Counting My Family

Here is Emma's family.

Draw yourself and your family.

How many people are in your family? _____

0 1 2 3 4 5 6 7 8 9 10

NOTE

Students count the number of people in their family.

MWI **Counting to 10**

Counting Quantities, Comparing Lengths

Counting Quantities,
Comparing Lengths

NAME   DATE

_____'s

Counting
Book

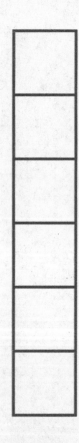

0

zero

1
one

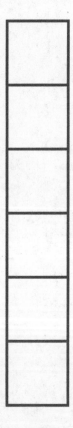

2
two

3
three

NAME

DATE

4

four

5
five

NAME

DATE

6
six

NAME   DATE

About the Mathematics in this Unit

Dear Family,

Our class is starting a new unit in mathematics called *Counting Quantities, Comparing Lengths*. The focus of this unit is on counting and comparing quantities and beginning to explore measurement by directly comparing objects to see which is longer.

Throughout this unit, students will be working toward these goals:

BENCHMARKS/GOALS	EXAMPLES
Count and count out a set of up to 10 objects.	How many buttons are there? "Can you count out 8 pencils?"
Describe length and decide which of two objects is longer.	Which is longer?

About the Mathematics in this Unit

BENCHMARKS/GOALS	EXAMPLES
Compare two quantities up to 10 to determine which is greater.	Are there more cars or shells?

In our math class, students engage in math problems and activities and discuss the underlying concepts. They are asked to share their reasoning and solutions. It is important that children solve math problems accurately in ways that make sense to them. At home, encourage your child to explain his or her math thinking to you.

In the coming weeks you will receive more information about this unit as well as suggestions for activities to do at home.

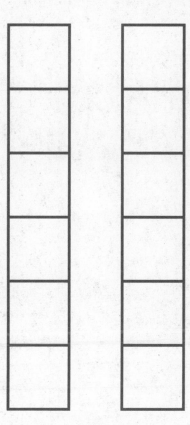

7
seven

NAME

DATE

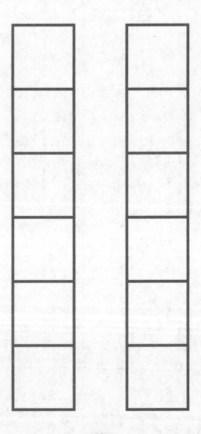

8
eight

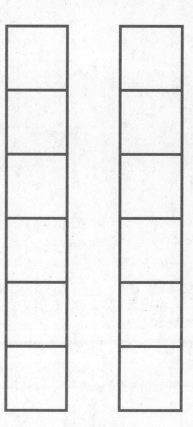

9
nine

NAME _____ DATE _____

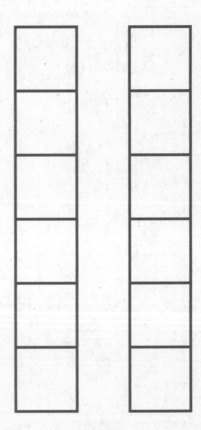

10
ten

NAME   DATE

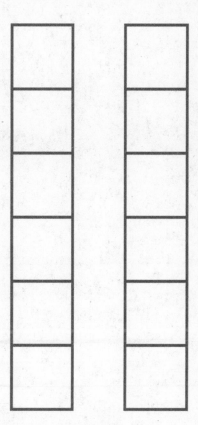

11
eleven

NAME

DATE

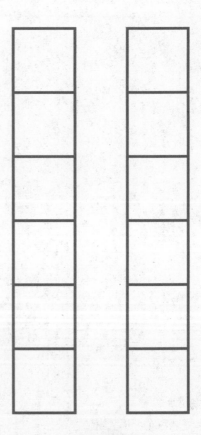

12
twelve

NAME _____ DATE _____

Fill the Number Cube

Fill in the dots on each number cube.

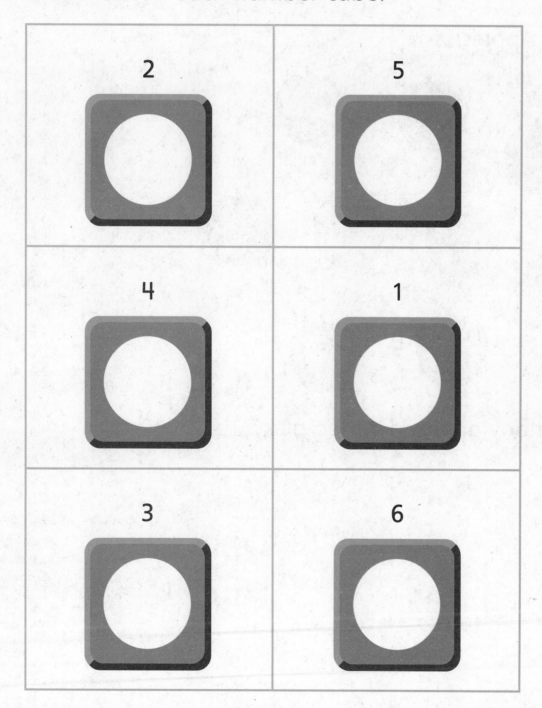

2	5
4	1
3	6

NOTE

Students draw dots to represent a given amount.
MWI Counting to 10

NAME

DATE

How Many Apples?

Count how many apples Meg picked.

Meg's Apples:

How many apples did Meg pick? _____

NOTE

Students practice counting and writing numbers.
MWI **Numbers 0 to 30**

NAME _____ DATE _____

Grab and Count

Mia played *Grab and Count*. How many did she grab?

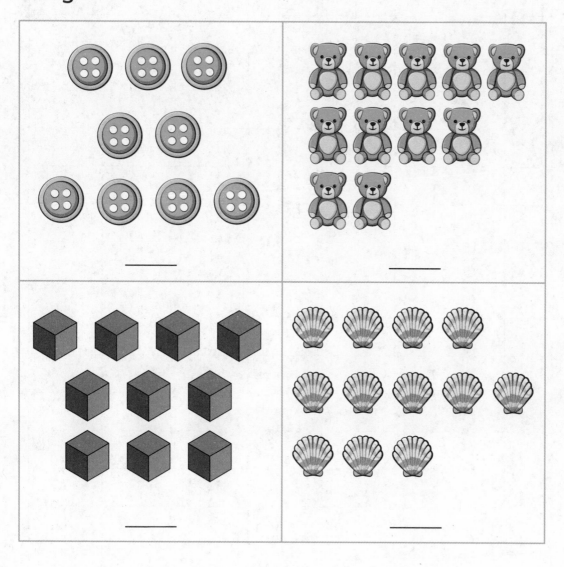

_____   _____

_____   _____

NOTE

Students have been playing Grab and Count at school.
MWI **Ways to Count**

© SAVVAS Learning Company LLC.

NAME

DATE

My Inventory Bag

Show what was in your bag.

Bag
_____

How many? _____

NAME

DATE

How Many Are There?

Jeff went shopping.
Draw how many things he got.

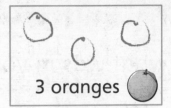

3 oranges

4 balls

7 apples

12 carrots

9 books

NOTE

Students draw pictures to represent a given amount.

MWI **How Many? (9–10)**

Longer or Shorter?

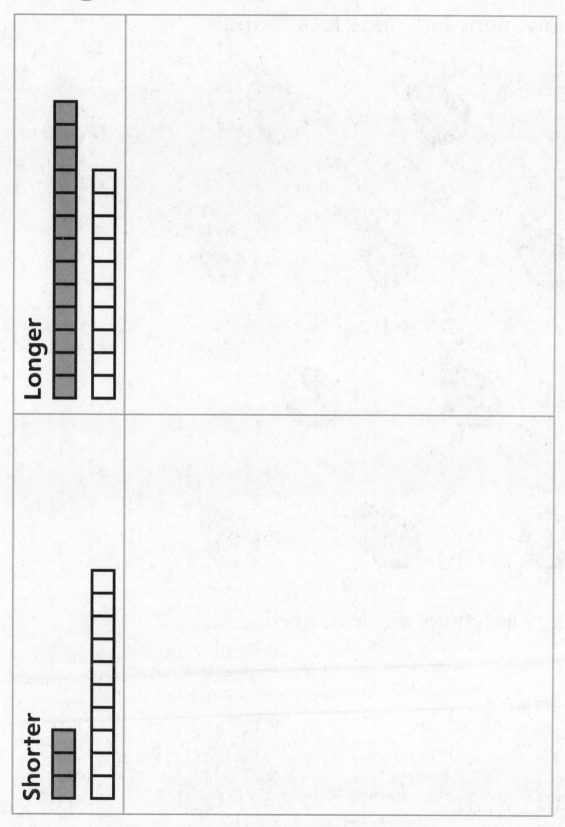

Longer

Shorter

NAME

DATE

How Many Ladybugs?

Count how many ladybugs Jack found.

How many ladybugs did Jack find? _____

NOTE

Students practice counting and writing numbers.
MWI **Numbers 0 to 30**

NAME   DATE

Related Activities to Try at Home

Dear Family,

The activities suggested below are related to the mathematics we are currently studying in school. Doing them together can enrich your child's mathematical learning.

Counting A major focus of this unit is counting. You can help your child learn to count fluently by finding many opportunities to ask your child to count in different ways. For example, sometimes count aloud together and see how high you can count. At other times, ask your child to count a small set of objects ("How many books are on the table?") or the number of pictures on a page. A slightly different kind of question is "Can you make a group of 6 blocks?" or "Can you count out 7 pennies?" You can also ask your child to count to solve a problem; for example, "If everyone needs a fork, how many forks do we need to set the table?"

Grab and Count Gather a set of objects, such as toy cars, blocks, or foam peanuts. Ask your child to grab a handful and count how many he or she grabbed. Then, ask your child to predict whether you will be able to grab more or less. Try it and find out. Your child can also grab two handfuls and see which holds more, the left hand or the right.

Related Activities

Which Is Longer? Another major focus of this unit is comparing objects to see which is longer. Find opportunities to ask your child about the length of different objects; for example, "What do you think the longest part of this cereal box is? Do you think the cereal box is longer than the milk carton? How could we find out?"

Playing *Compare* We have been playing a card game called *Compare* that is similar to the familiar card game, *War*. You could play at home with a deck of playing cards. Each player gets half of a deck of cards and puts them in a pile facedown. Both players turn over their top card, and the person with the greater number says, "Me." Ask your child to explain how he or she knows which number is greater. The game is over when all of the cards have been turned over.

Math and Literature You can find the following counting books in your local library and read them together. Ask your child to count the objects on each page, and see what mathematical concepts your child discovers.

- Bowman, Anne. *Count Them While You Can...: A Book of Endangered Animals.*
- Gayzagian, Doris. *One White Wishing Stone: A Beach Day Counting Book.*
- Krebs, Laurie. *We All Went on Safari: A Counting Journey Through Tanzania.*
- Mora, Pat. *Uno, Dos, Tres: One, Two, Three.*
- Martin, Bill. *Chicka Chicka 1, 2, 3.*
- Wormell, Christopher. *Teeth, Tails, and Tentacles.*

NAME   DATE

Longer or Shorter Than My Hand

Compare the length of objects at home to
your hand. Draw the objects.

Shorter than my hand	Longer than my hand

NOTE

In class, students have been comparing the length of two objects to see which is longer.
Tonight students compare the length of objects at home to their hand. They draw or make a
list of objects that are longer than their hand and shorter than their hand.

MWI **Shorter Than or Longer Than**

Which Is Longer?

Circle the picture that is longer.

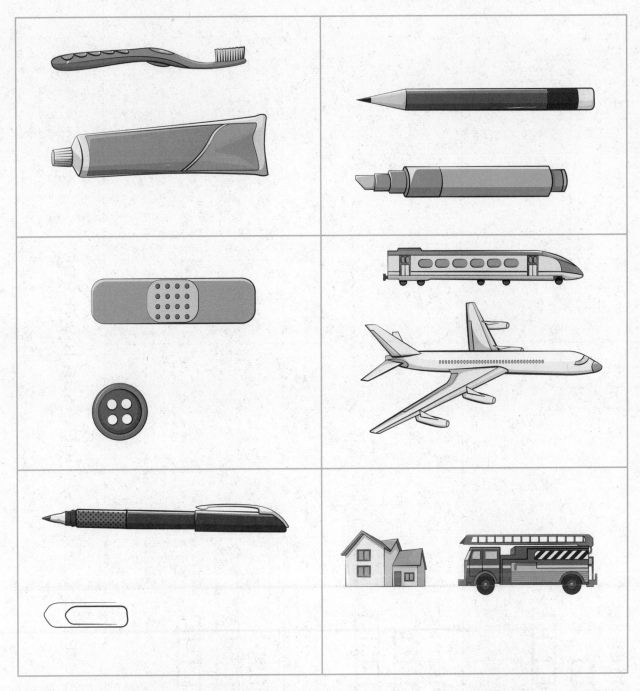

NOTE

Students compare pictures of two objects to determine which is longer.
MWI **Shorter Than or Longer Than**

NAME

DATE

Comparing Names

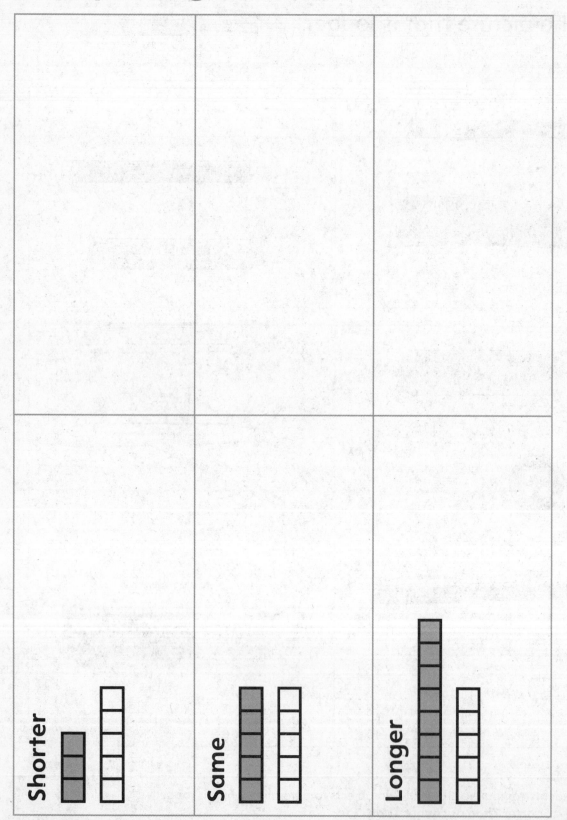

There are _____ letters in my name.

NAME _____ DATE _____

Names at Home

Write the names of people at home.
Circle the name with the most letters.

Corey
Mom
Gram
(Patrick)
Cait

Name	How Many Letters?
_____	_____
_____	_____
_____	_____
_____	_____
_____	_____
_____	_____

NOTE

In class, students counted the number of letters in their names and compared names to find out which are longer and shorter. Tonight, students count and compare the number of letters in the names of the people at home.

MWI **One More and One Fewer**

NAME

DATE

Snacks

Mia has 9 friends at her house for a party.
She wants to give them each one snack.
She has these snacks.

Does she have enough apples for everyone?
How do you know?

NOTE

Students count and compare numbers.
MWI **More; Fewer**

Make a Shape, Fill a Hexagon

Make a Shape,
Fill a Hexagon

About the Mathematics in This Unit

Dear Family,

We are beginning a new unit in mathematics called *Make a Shape, Fill a Hexagon.* This geometry unit focuses on two-dimensional shapes. In this unit, students look for and identify two-dimensional shapes in their environment and make a Class Book of Shapes and a Shape Mural using geometric shapes to depict the objects they see. They look carefully at the attributes of shapes as they describe, identify, compare, construct, and represent 2-D shapes. Students also combine shapes to make new shapes (e.g., 2 trapezoids make a hexagon).

Throughout this unit, students will be working toward these goals:

Benchmarks/Goals	Examples
Identify and describe the overall size, shape, and features of familiar 2-D shapes.	"It has a triangle on one side." "It's big." "It would make a good ramp." "It looks like a piece of pie." "One part is pointy."
Make 2-D shapes.	

About the Mathematics in This Unit

Benchmarks/Goals	Examples
Combine shapes to make 2-D shapes.	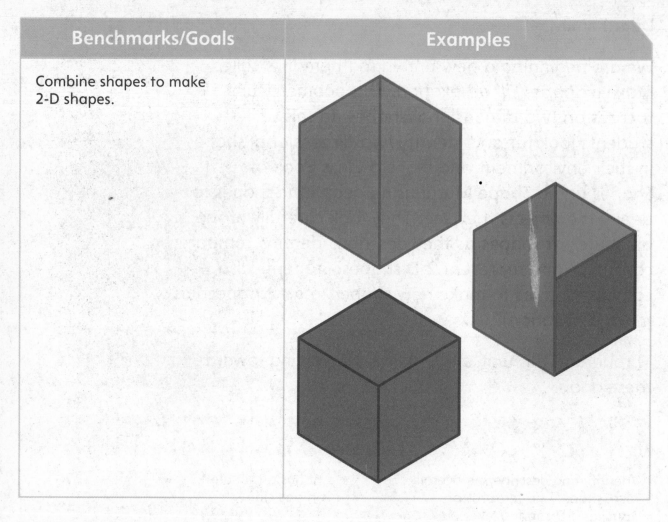

In our math class, students engage in math problems and activities and discuss the underlying concepts. They are asked to share their reasoning and solutions. It is important that children solve math problems accurately in ways that make sense to them. At home, encourage your child to explain his or her math thinking to you.

In the coming weeks, you will receive information about activities to do at home.

NAME

DATE

Color the Shapes

Color all of the squares ☐ blue.

Color all of the triangles △ red.

How many squares did you color? _____

How many triangles did you color? _____

NOTE

Students practice identifying squares and triangles.
MWI **Geometry and Shapes in the World**

Related Activities to Try at Home

Dear Family,

The activities below are related to the mathematics in the geometry unit *Make a Shape, Fill a Hexagon*. Doing them at home together with your child can enrich your child's mathematical learning.

Shape Hunt Shapes are everywhere. Talk with your child about the shapes you see every day. Together, you can look at everything from the shapes of buildings in your neighborhood to the shapes of boxes and cans in the supermarket. Sometimes you can include descriptions of shapes in what you say. For example, "Look at that part of the building shaped like a trapezoid." At other times, you can ask your child to look for specific shapes: "See how many things you can find that are triangles, while we walk down the street."

Making Shapes Making shapes is a great way to learn about them. At home, your child might use clay, drinking straws, or a loop of yarn or rope to make different shapes.

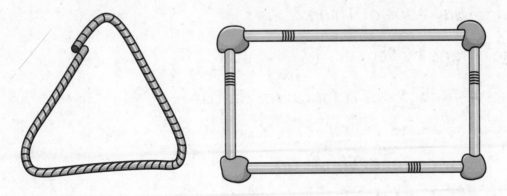

Ask your child, "Can you make a shape with three sides? . . . Do you know what that shape is called?" Or, you can make different shapes and ask your child to name and describe them.

Related Activities to Try at Home

Drawing Shapes Drawing shapes is also fun. In class we have been making a class book of shapes and a shape mural. Your child might like to design his or her own shape book, picture, or mural using many different shapes that he or she has drawn or cut from old magazines.

Seeing Shapes Inside Shapes Encourage your child to look for patterns or designs made from different shapes. For example, ask: "Can you find squares on the floor (or wallpaper or clothing)?" or "Are there any patterns made from triangles?" or "Do you see any hexagons?"

Math and Literature Here are some suggestions of children's books that contain relevant ideas about geometry. Read them together and talk about the shapes you find.

Blackstone, Stella. *Ship Shapes*.

Burns, Marilyn. *The Greedy Triangle*.

Dodds, Dayle Ann. *The Shape of Things*.

MacDonald, Suse. *Shape by Shape*.

Onyefulu, Ifeoma. *A Triangle for Adaora: An African Book of Shapes*.

Schachner, Judy. *Skippyjon Jones Shape Up*.

The Metropolitan Museum of Art. *Museum Shapes*.

Thong, Roseanne. *Round Is a Mooncake*.

NAME

DATE

Sorting Buttons

What's the same about the buttons in the circle?

Draw arrows to show the other buttons that belong.

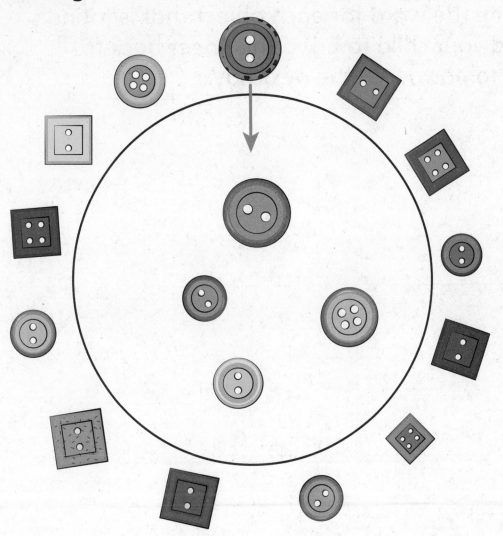

How many other buttons belong in the circle? _____

NOTE

Students sort buttons based on a particular attribute.

MWI **Sorting Buttons**

Shape Hunt at Home

Dear Family,

Your child will be looking for objects in your home that contain these shapes. For example, a door is shaped like a rectangle. After your child draws the object, you can help your child write the word for each object that is found. Please remind your child to bring this sheet back to school either tomorrow or the next day.

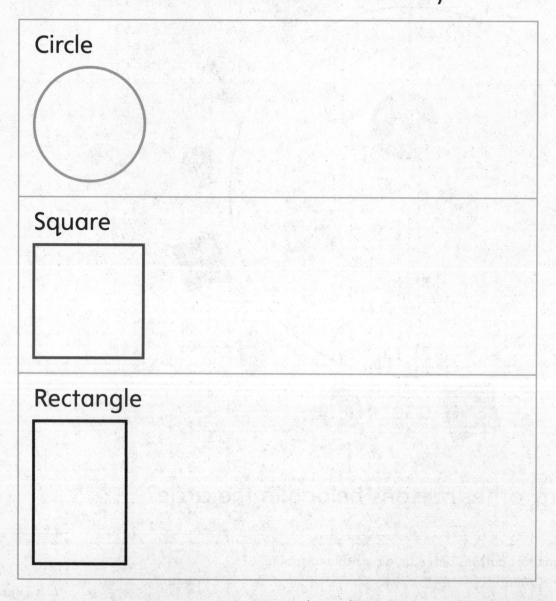

Circle

Square

Rectangle

NAME

DATE

Shape Hunt at Home

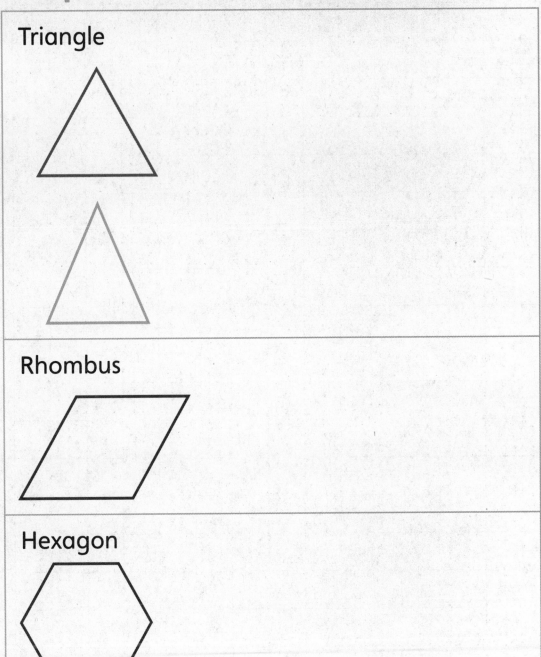

Triangle

Rhombus

Hexagon

NOTE

Students look for shapes and draw objects containing these shapes.
MWI **Geometry and Shapes in the World**

NAME   DATE

How Many Pattern Block Shapes?

Color the triangles △ green.

Color the rhombuses ▱ blue.

Color the trapezoids ⏢ red.

Color the hexagons ⬡ yellow.

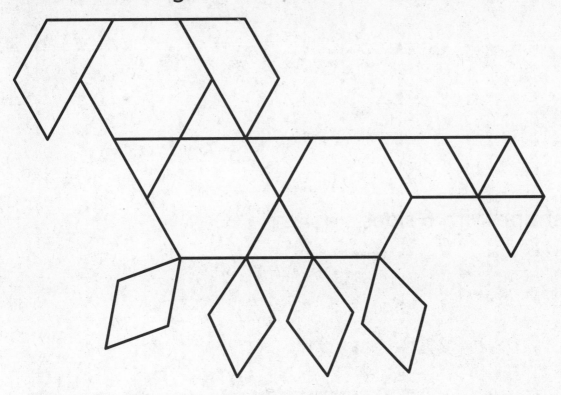

Shape	⬡	▲	◢	■	╱	▲	Total
How Many?							

NOTE

Students count and record the number of each pattern block shape.
MWI Pattern Block Puzzles

NAME

DATE

Can You Draw It?

Draw these shapes. Use the dot paper
to help you or to draw more shapes.

1 A shape with 3 sides

2 A shape with 4 sides

3 A shape with 6 sides

NAME

DATE

Dot Paper

NOTE

Students create 2-D shapes by drawing lines to connect the dots.

MWI Types of 2-D Shapes

Collect, Count,
and Measure

Collect, Count, and Measure

About the Mathematics in This Unit

Dear Family,

Our class is starting a new unit in mathematics called *Collect, Count, and Measure*. The focus of this unit is on counting and measuring. Students line up craft sticks or cubes to measure the length of objects, including the length of their shoes. They develop visual images for quantities up to 10 as they roll dot cubes, work with Ten Frames, and find many different ways to arrange and describe a set of 5 to 10 tiles.

 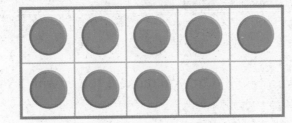 

Students count and compare quantities throughout this unit. These activities support students as they make connections between counting and combining, which helps them begin to add and subtract small numbers. For example, they solve simple story problems and play games that ask them to figure out the total when 1, 2, and 3 are added or when 1 is taken away.

About the Mathematics in This Unit

Throughout this unit, students will be working toward these goals:

Benchmarks/Goals	Examples
Count, and count out, a set of up to 15 objects.	How many pennies are there? Can you make a tower with 15 cubes?
Figure out what is one more or one less than a number.	What's 1 more than 5? 5

In our math class, students engage in math problems and activities and discuss the underlying concepts. They are asked to share their reasoning and solutions. It is important that children solve math problems accurately in ways that make sense to them. At home, encourage your child to explain his or her math thinking to you.

In the coming weeks, you will receive information about activities to do at home.

NAME

DATE

Measuring Shoes

1 I measured _____'s shoe.

It was _____ cubes long.

2 I measured _____'s shoe.

It was _____ cubes long.

3 I measured _____'s shoe.

It was _____ cubes long.

4 I measured _____'s shoe.

It was _____ cubes long.

5 I measured _____'s shoe.

It was _____ cubes long.

NAME

DATE

Trace a Shoe at Home

Dear Family,

At school we have been making outlines of our shoes to measure how long they are. Students are excited to add more shoes!

Please help your child find a shoe that doesn't belong to them. Put the shoe in the space below, and trace around the edges. (If it's a very large shoe, you might need to tape 2 pieces of paper together.) Then, help your child write the owner's name on the outline.

Feel free to trace as many different shoes as you like!

NOTE

Students trace outlines of shoes on paper.
MWI Things We Measure

NAME _____   DATE _____

Measuring with Sticks

We measured with this: ⬭⬭⬭

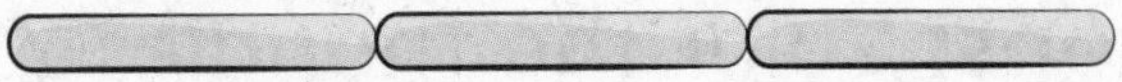

1 I measured Strip _____.

It was _____ sticks long.

2 I measured Strip _____.

It was _____ sticks long.

3 I measured Strip _____.

It was _____ sticks long.

4 I measured Strip _____.

It was _____ sticks long.

5 I measured Strip _____.

It was _____ sticks long.

NAME

DATE

How Many Pattern Block Shapes? 2

Directions: Color the triangles △ green.

Color the rhombuses ▱ blue.

Color the trapezoids ⬯ red.

Color the hexagons ⬡ yellow.

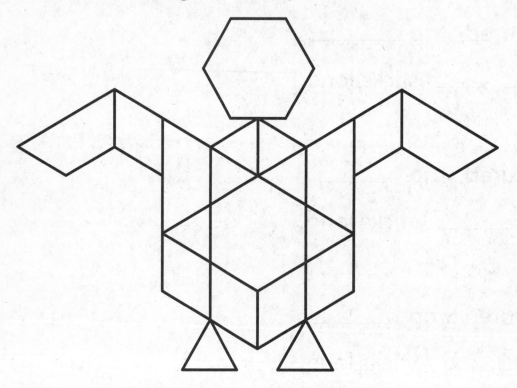

Shape	⬢	◣	◢	▪	╱	▲	Total
How Many?				0	0		

NOTE

Students count and record the number of each pattern block shape.
MWI Pattern Block Puzzles

NAME _____   DATE _____

Measuring with Cubes ▪●●●●●●●●●●●●●▪

1   I measured the _____.

It was _____ cubes long.

2   I measured the _____.

It was _____ cubes long.

3   I measured the _____.

It was _____ cubes long.

4   I measured the _____.

It was _____ cubes long.

5   I measured the _____.

It was _____ cubes long.

NAME

DATE

How Many?

Record how many.

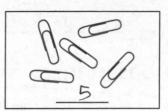

5

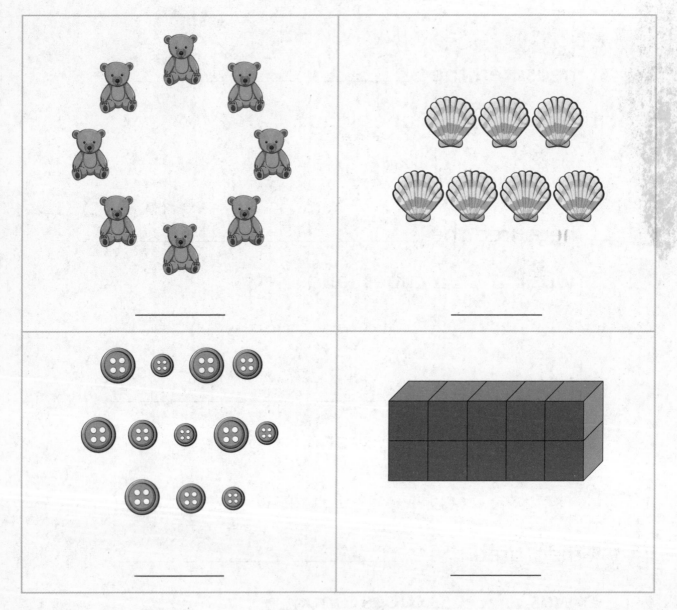

_____

_____

_____

_____

NOTE

Students practice counting and writing numbers.
MWI Counting to 10

NAME

DATE

Measuring Pictures

Record how many tiles long each object is.

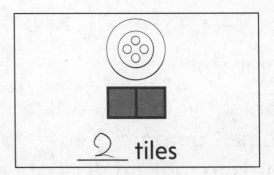

_2_ tiles

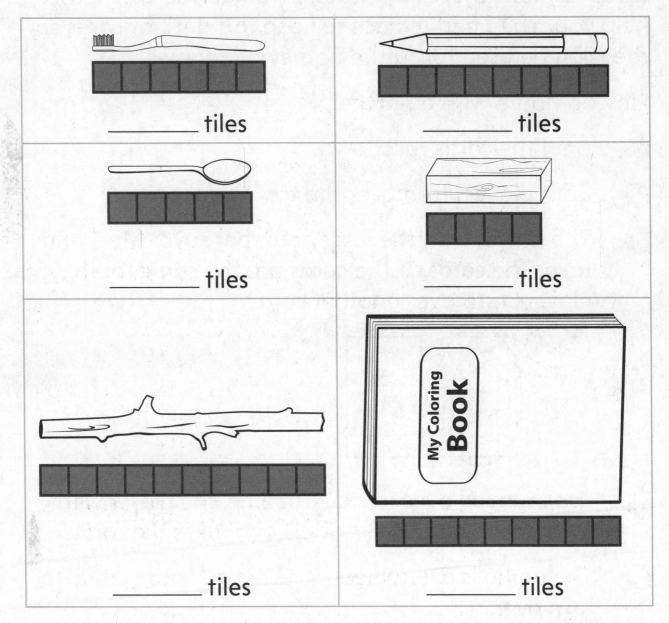

_____ tiles

_____ tiles

_____ tiles

_____ tiles

_____ tiles

_____ tiles

NOTE

Students practice counting and measuring objects using cubes, a nonstandard measuring tool.

MWI Measuring With Cubes

NAME _____ DATE _____

Compare at Home

Dear Family,

Tonight your child will teach you how to play the card game *Compare*. Please cut apart the attached set of cards to make a deck of Primary Number Cards. Please help your child find a place to keep this deck of cards so they can be used for future homework games.

Play *Compare* with a partner.

1. Deal the cards facedown.

2. Both players turn over the top card.

3. The player with the larger number says "Me!" and takes the cards. If the cards are the same, both players turn over another card.

4. Keep turning over cards. Each time, the player with the larger number says "Me!" and takes the cards.

5. The game is over when there are no more cards to turn over.

NOTE

Students compare two numbers and determine which is larger.
MWI More

NAME   DATE

Quick Images

Record the total number of dots.

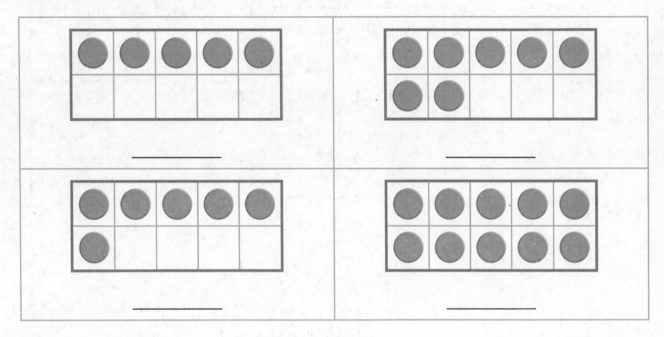

Draw dots to show the number.

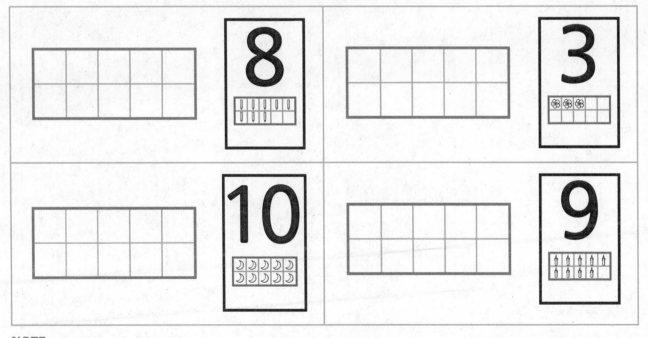

NOTE

Students record the total number shown on the Ten Frame and represent a given number on a Ten Frame.

MWI Ten Frames

Related Activities to Try at Home

Dear Family,

The activities suggested below are related to the mathematics we are currently studying in school. Doing them with your child can enrich your child's mathematical learning.

Measuring Shoes In school, we have been using cubes to measure the length of our shoes. Your child may enjoy investigating the length of shoes at home. Just as we do in school, your child can trace shoe outlines on paper, and then use paper clips (or another same-sized item such as blocks or toothpicks) to measure the length of the outline. Ask your child to put the shoe lengths in order from the shortest to the longest.

Counting We continue to focus on strategies for counting accurately. At home, find many ways to count together with your child; for example, count aloud, count sets of objects, ask your child to count out specific amounts, and pose problems that he or she can solve by counting. The list of suggested books below includes several counting books that you can read together.

One More or Less Find opportunities to ask your child about one more and one less, an idea we have been working on in class. For example, after your child counts a set of objects such as pennies, ask, "What if I gave you one more penny? Then how many would you have?" or "What if I took one penny back? Then how many would you have?" Then, add (or remove) a penny. That way, your child can recount the set from one to find out or to double-check the answer.

Many counting books that count up from one (i.e., from 1 to 10) present situations of "one more"; books that count back (i.e., from 10 to 1) present situations of "one less." (See list of books.)

Related Activities to Try at Home

Playing *Double Compare* We have been playing a card game called *Double Compare* that is similar to the familiar card game, *War*. This game uses the cards 0–6. You could play at home with a deck of playing cards. Each player gets half the deck and puts the cards in a pile, facedown. Both players turn over their top two cards, and the person with the larger total says, "Me." Ask your child to explain how he or she knows which total is greater. The game is over when all of the cards have been turned over.

Math and Literature You can find these books in your local library and read them together. These books focus on measuring, counting forward, and counting back.

Books About Measuring

Murphy, Stuart J. *Super Sand Castle Saturday*.

Counting Forward

Krebs, Laurie. *We All Went on Safari: A Counting Journey Through Tanzania*.
Mora, Pat. *Uno, Dos, Tres, One, Two, Three*.
Wormell, Christopher. *Teeth, Tails and Tentacles: An Animal Counting Book*.

Counting Back

Dale, Penny. *Ten in Bed*.
Murphy, Stuart J. *Monster Musical Chairs*.
Wise, William. *Ten Sly Piranhas*.

NAME _____ DATE _____

Grab and Count at Home: Two Handfuls

Dear Family,

Tonight your child will teach you how to play *Grab and Count: Two Handfuls.* You will need a container of small objects, such as small blocks, bottle caps, pennies, buttons or small blocks.

What did you grab? _____
How many did you grab? _____
Show how many.

NAME   DATE

Grab and Count at Home:
Two Handfuls

What did you grab? _____

How many did you grab? _____

Show how many.

NOTE

Students count and record numbers of objects.
MWI Counting to 10

NAME

DATE

Double Compare

Circle the pair of cards in each row that shows more.

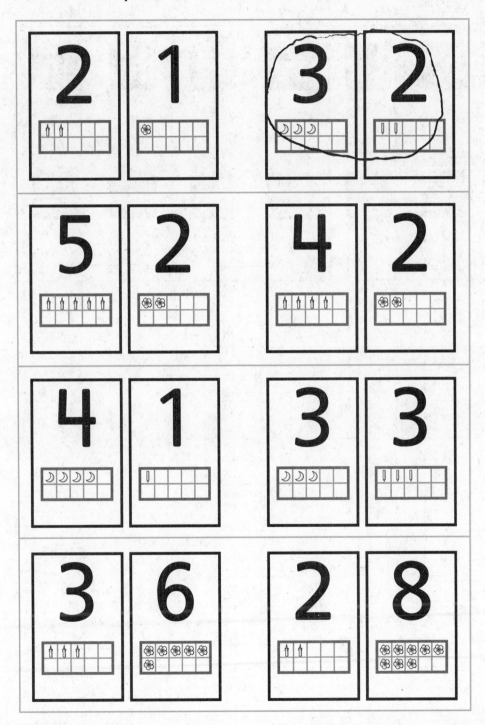

NOTE

Students combine two amounts and determine which total is greater.
MWI **More**

NAME _____ DATE _____

Roll and Record 2

Write the total.

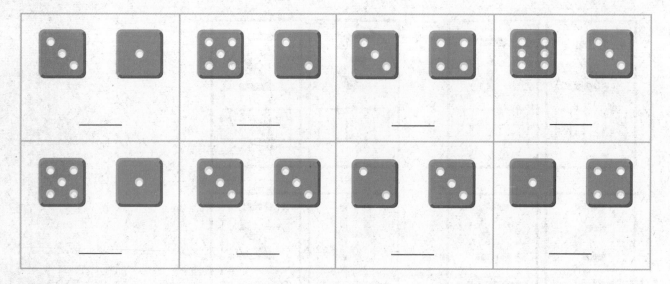

_____	_____	_____	_____
_____	_____	_____	_____

Record each total on the grid.

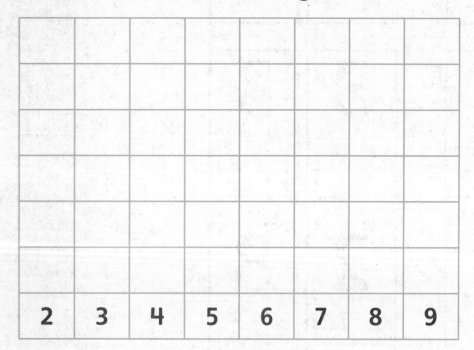

| 2 | 3 | 4 | 5 | 6 | 7 | 8 | 9 |

NOTE

Students combine two amounts and record the total.
MWI Ways to Make Six

NAME

DATE

Double Compare at Home

Dear Family,

Tonight your child will teach you how to play the card game *Double Compare*.

Double Compare

You need

- Deck of Primary Number Cards (without Wild Cards)

Play with a partner.

1. Deal the cards facedown.

2. Both players turn over their top two cards.

3. The player with the larger total says "Me!" and takes the cards. If the totals are the same, both players turn over two more cards.

4. Keep turning over two cards. Each time, the player with the larger total says "Me!" and takes the cards.

5. The game is over when there are no more cards to turn over.

More Ways to Play

- The player with the **smaller** total says "Me!"
- Play with 3 players.
- Play with the Wild Cards. A Wild Card can be any number.

NOTE

Students combine two amounts and determine which total is greater.
MWI Fewer

NAME

DATE

Inch Grid Paper

NAME _____   DATE _____

Double Compare

Circle the pair of cards in each row that shows more.

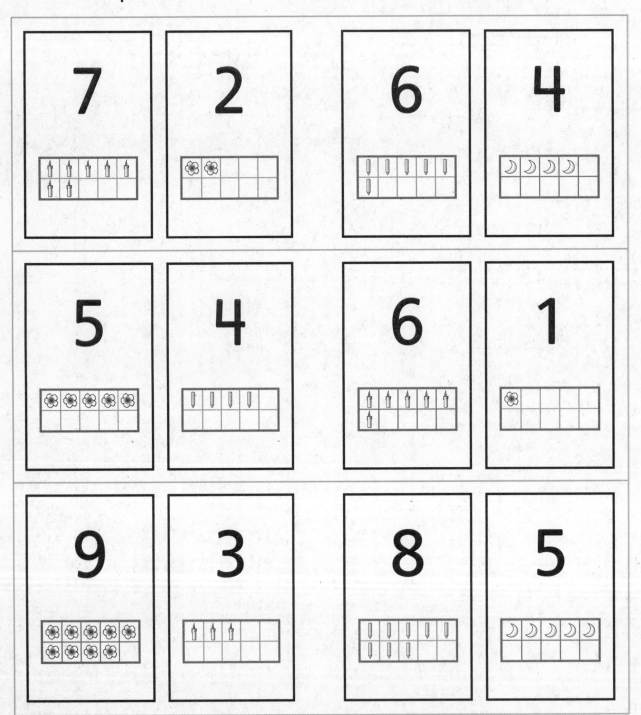

NOTE

Students combine two amounts and determine which total is greater.

MWI More

NAME

DATE

How Many Tiles?

How many tiles are there?
Show how you know.

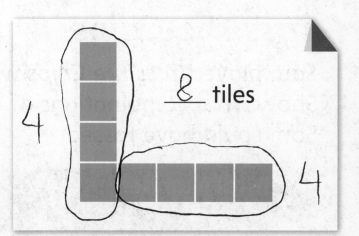

4   _&_ tiles   4

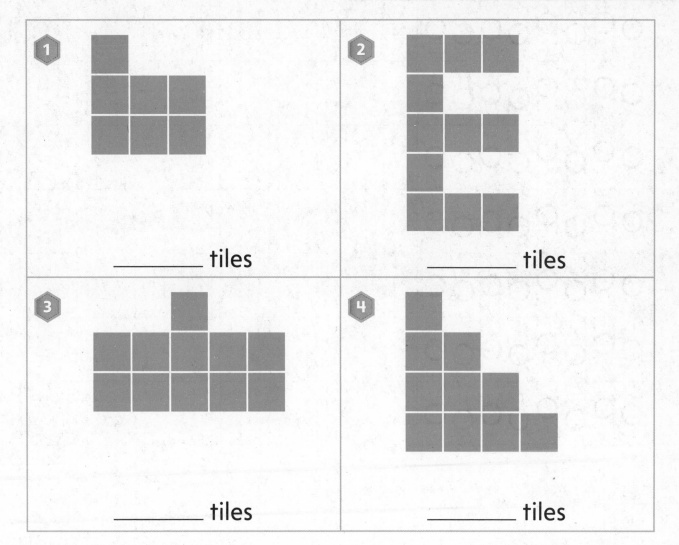

1

_____ tiles

2

_____ tiles

3

_____ tiles

4

_____ tiles

NOTE

Students break a quantity into parts and find the total.
MWI Arranging Five Tiles

NAME   DATE

Toss the Chips: 8

Sam played *Toss the Chips* with 8 counters.
Show what combinations of red and yellow
Sam could have tossed.

Total Number 8	Red	Yellow
⚪⚪⚪⚪⚪⚪⚪⚪		
⚪⚪⚪⚪⚪⚪⚪⚪		
⚪⚪⚪⚪⚪⚪⚪⚪		
⚪⚪⚪⚪⚪⚪⚪⚪		
⚪⚪⚪⚪⚪⚪⚪⚪		
⚪⚪⚪⚪⚪⚪⚪⚪		
⚪⚪⚪⚪⚪⚪⚪⚪		

NOTE

Students practice counting and breaking a number into two parts.
MWI A Story Problem About How Many of Each?

Build a Block,
Build a Wall

Build a Block,
Build a Wall

3-D Shape Hunt

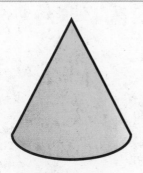

Cone

Sphere

Rectangular Prism

Cube

3-D Shape Hunt

Cylinder

Triangular Prism

Square Prism

Pyramid

NAME	DATE

About the Mathematics in This Unit

Dear Family,

We are beginning a new unit in mathematics called *Build a Block, Build a Wall*. This geometry unit focuses on three-dimensional shapes. In this unit, students look for and identify three-dimensional shapes in the real-world as they go on Shape Hunts in school and at home. They create, identify, describe, compare, represent, and build with 3-D shapes. They also explore the relationship between 2-D and 3-D shapes as they match the faces of Geoblocks—a set of related three-dimensional wooden blocks—to corresponding 2-D shapes.

Throughout this unit, students will be working toward these goals:

Benchmarks/Goals	Examples
Understand words that describe relative position.	• above • on top of • below • beneath • beside • next to • in front of • behind
Identify and describe the overall size, shape, and features of familiar 3-D shapes.	"It has a triangle on one side." "It's big." "It would make a good ramp." "It looks like a piece of pie." "One part is pointy."
Make 3-D shapes.	
Combine shapes to make 3-D shapes.	

About the Mathematics in This Unit

In our math class, students engage in math problems and activities and discuss the underlying concepts. They are asked to share their reasoning and solutions. It is important that children solve math problems accurately in ways that make sense to them. At home, encourage your child to explain his or her math thinking to you.

In the coming weeks, you will receive more information about this unit as well as suggestions for activities to do at home.

3-D Shape Hunt at Home

Dear Family,

Your child will be going on a Shape Hunt
at home to look for real-world objects that
look like these three-dimensional shapes.
As you hunt for shapes with your child,
help them record the name of each object.

Sphere

Cylinder

NOTE

Students identify and record names of objects that look like 3-D shapes.
MWI **Geometry and Shapes in the World**

NAME   DATE

3-D Shape Hunt at Home

Cube

Cone

Rectangular Prism

Related Activities to Try at Home

Dear Family,

The activities below are related to the mathematics in the geometry unit, *Build a Block, Build a Wall*. Doing them at home together with your child can enrich your child's mathematical learning.

3-D Shape Hunt Shapes are everywhere. Talk with your child about the shapes you see every day. Together, you can look at everything from the shapes of buildings in your neighborhood, to the shapes of boxes and cans in the supermarket. Sometimes you can include descriptions of shapes in what you say. For example, "Look at that part of the building that is shaped like a cylinder." At other times, you can ask your child to look for specific shapes: "See how many things you can find that are shaped like a cube while we walk down the street."

Making Shapes Making shapes is a great way to learn about them. At home, your child might use clay, building blocks, drinking straws and clay, or other types of construction toys or materials to make different shapes.

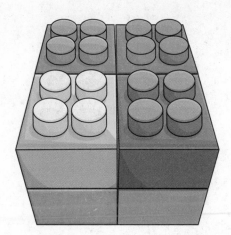

Ask your child, "Can you make a cube? How many faces (sides) does it have?" "Can you make a shape that looks like this shoebox?" Or, you can make different shapes and ask your child to describe and copy them.

Related Activities to Try at Home

Drawing Shapes While it is difficult to draw 3-D shapes, some students enjoy the challenge. Talk together about ways to draw a shape so that it "looks 3-D" and practice.

Math and Literature Here are some suggestions of children's books that contain relevant ideas about geometry. Read them together and talk about the shapes you find.

Hoban, Tana. *Cubes, Cones, Cylinders and Spheres.*

Murphy, Stuart J. *Captain Invincible and the Space Shapes.*

Nagel, Karen. *Shapes that Roll.*

Onyefulu, Ifeoma. *A Triangle for Adaora: An African Book of Shapes.*

Thong, Rosanne. *Round is a Mooncake: A Book of Shapes.*

NAME

DATE

Matching Blocks to Faces

Match each GeoBlock to a GeoBlock footprint.

GeoBlocks   **Footprints**

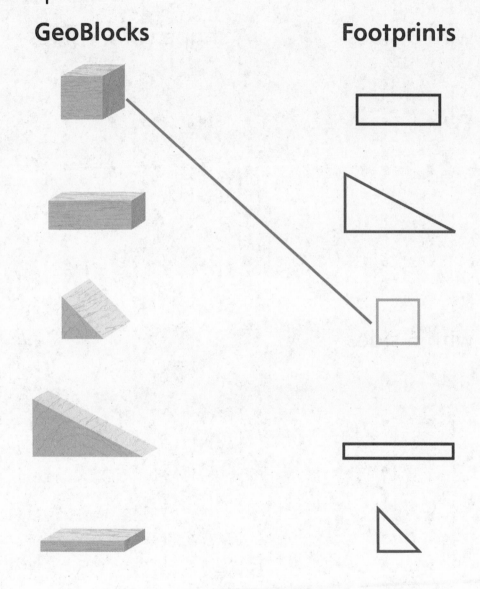

NOTE

Students match one face of a 3-D object to a 2-D shape.
MWI **Matching GeoBlock Faces**

NAME

DATE

Can You Draw It?

Draw these shapes. Use the dot paper
to help you or to draw more shapes.

1 A shape with 3 sides

2 A shape with 4 sides

3 A shape with 6 sides

NOTE

Students draw shapes with specific attributes.
MWI **Types of 2-D Shapes**

UNIT 5 | 100 | SESSION 1.9   © SAVVAS Learning Company LLC.

NAME

DATE

Dot Paper

NOTE

Students practice drawing 2-D shapes.
MWI **Geometry and Shapes in the World**

UNIT 5 | 101 | SESSION 1.9   © SAVVAS Learning Company LLC.

How Many Now?

How Many Now?

NAME _____   DATE _____

Measuring Ourselves Part 1

Me ___ NAME	Measure this Body Part	My Friend ___ NAME

About the Mathematics in This Unit

Dear Family,

Our class is starting a new unit in mathematics called *How Many Now?* The focus of this unit is on combinations, counting, and addition and subtraction. Students record different ways a set of two-color counters can land, figure out how many blue and red crayons could be in a set of five crayons, and play a card game in which they look for combinations of cards that total six. All of these activities focus on the idea that one number can be broken apart in many ways: 6 is 3 and 3 or 5 and 1 or 2 and 2 and 2. Students also count sets of up to 20 objects, and continue making sense of addition and subtraction through story problems and games that ask them to combine or separate small amounts.

Throughout this unit, students will be working toward these goals:

Benchmarks/Goals	Examples
Count and count out a set of up to 20 objects.	How many pennies are there? Can you make a tower with 20 cubes?
Write the numbers to 10.	How many are red? How many are yellow? | Red	Yellow | | 2 | 4 |

About the Mathematics in This Unit

Benchmarks/Goals	Examples
Represent and solve addition problems within 10.	How many counters should Mia take? $\underline{3} + \underline{4} = 7$ Jack had 6 blocks. Carmen gave him 2 more. How many blocks did Jack have then? ⑧
Decompose a number into two addends in more than one way.	I have 6 crayons in all. Some are red and some are blue. How many of each could I have? How many blues? How many reds? 4 blue 2 red 1 blue 5 red

In our math class, students engage in math problems and activities and discuss the underlying concepts. They are asked to share their reasoning and solutions. It is important that children solve math problems accurately in ways that make sense to them. At home, encourage your child to explain his or her math thinking to you.

In the coming weeks, you will receive information about activities to do at home.

NAME _____ DATE _____

Counting on the Number Line

Write the missing numbers on the number line.

1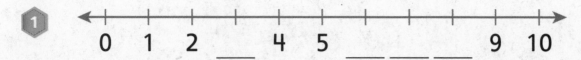

0 1 2 ___ 4 5 ___ ___ ___ 9 10

2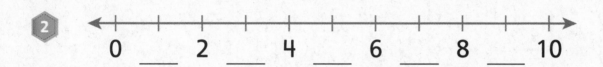

0 ___ 2 ___ 4 ___ 6 ___ 8 ___ 10

3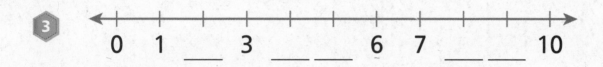

0 1 ___ 3 ___ ___ 6 7 ___ ___ 10

4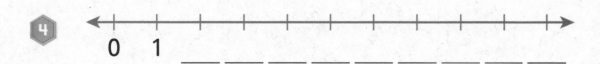

0 1 ___ ___ ___ ___ ___ ___ ___ ___

NOTE

Students practice writing numbers and counting.
MWI Counting on the Number Line

NAME _____ DATE _____

My Inventory Bag

Show what was in your bag.

Bag

___

How many? _____

NAME

DATE

Inventory Bag

Count the number of crayons, markers, and pencils.

Count how many there are in all.

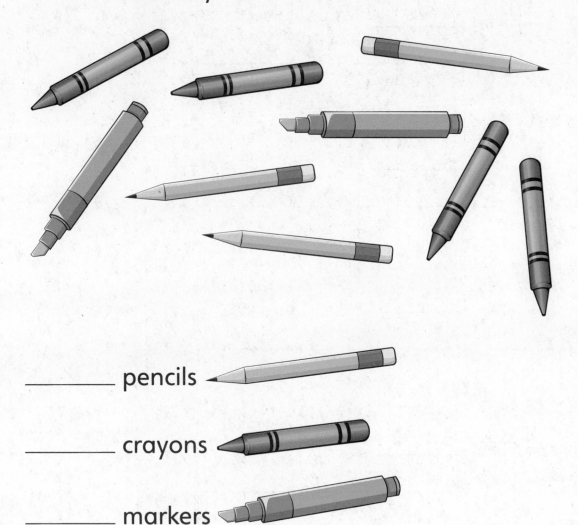

_____ pencils

_____ crayons

_____ markers

How many are there in all? _____

NOTE

Students practice counting and writing numbers.
MWI How Many? (9–10)

NAME

DATE

Roll and Record

Write the total.

<table>
<tr><td>⚁ one dot / ⚀ ⚀</td><td>2</td></tr>
<tr><td>⚂ ⚄</td><td>___</td></tr>
<tr><td>⚁ ⚀</td><td>___</td></tr>
<tr><td>⚀ ⚂</td><td>___</td></tr>
<tr><td>⚃ ⚁</td><td>___</td></tr>
</table>

NOTE

Students combine two amounts to find the total.
MWI **How Many? (0–6); How Many? (7–8)**

UNIT 6 | 112 | SESSION 2.3

© SAVVAS Learning Company LLC.

NAME _____ DATE _____

Inventories at Home

Dear Family,

Your child will be taking an "inventory" of a related set of objects at home. Examples might be: a collection of stuffed animals, toy cars, books, or a set of items from the kitchen such as silverware or canned goods. They should count each type of item, for example: 4 red cars, 5 black cars, 2 green cars; count how many in all, and record all the information below or on the back of this page.

What did you Inventory? _____

How many objects were in your Inventory? _____

Show how many.

NOTE

Students count related sets of objects.
MWI **Numbers 0 to 30**

UNIT 6 | 113 | SESSION 2.5   © SAVVAS Learning Company LLC.

NAME

DATE

How Many Blocks?

Solve the problem. Show your work.

Jack was building with blocks.
He used 2 blocks to build a wall.
He used 4 blocks to build a bridge.

How many blocks did Jack use?

Related Activities to Try at Home

Dear Family,

The activities suggested below are related to the mathematics we are currently studying in school. Doing them with your child can enrich your child's mathematical learning.

Counting We continue to focus on strategies for counting accurately and are practicing counting sets of up to 20 objects. This is more challenging because there are more objects to keep track of, but also because the number sequence in the teens doesn't follow the same pattern as the rest of the numbers. For example, think about 21, 22, 23 (or 31, 32, 33 or 41, 42, 43), and then consider the fact that we don't say ten-one, ten-two, ten-three for 11, 12, 13. You can support your child by finding lots of ways to count together at home.

Solving Story Problems In this unit, students have many opportunities to solve problems about combining (addition) and separating (subtraction) small amounts. At home, find ways to present problems about common situations: "There are six people in our family. But Grandma and Grandpa are joining us for dinner tonight. How many people will there be?". Or, "Usually, we have six people at our dinner table, but José is eating at a friend's house. How many people will there be?". Or, "If James wants three tacos, and Maria wants four, how many tacos do I need to make?". Encourage children to explain how they solve such problems. Most kindergarteners count from one. Some may count on (or back) or "just know" some combinations.

Related Activities to Try at Home

Playing Double Compare We have been playing *Double Compare* with all of the cards from 0 to 10. You could play at home with a deck of playing cards. Each player gets half the deck. Both players turn over their top two cards, and the person with the greater total says "me." The game is over when all of the cards have been turned over. Be sure to ask your child to explain how she or he knows which number is greater. You might be surprised—although many children count or add to find and compare the totals, some children do not. Instead they reason about the numbers:

"I have 6 and 3. You have 6 and 5. We both have 6, so you have more because 5 is more than 3."

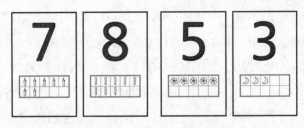

"Both of my numbers are bigger than both of yours. So I have more."

Or, "I have 2 big numbers, and you have 2 small numbers. I have more."

Math and Literature You can find these books in your local library and read them together. These books focus on measuring, counting forward, and counting back:

Bang, Molly. *Ten, Nine, Eight*.

Dale, Penny. *Ten in the Bed*.

Bowman, Anne. *Count Them While you Can…: A Book of Endangered Animals*.

Deitz Shea, Pegi, Cynthia Weill, and Pahm Viet-Dinh. *Ten Mice for Tet!*

Heo, Yeumi. *Ten Days and Nine Nights: An Adoption Story*.

Martin, Bill. *Chicka Chicka 1, 2, 3*.

Metropolitan Museum of Art. *Museum 123*.

Sayre, April Pulley and Sayre, Jeff. *One is a Snail, Ten is a Crab*.

NAME

DATE

How Many Grapes?

Read the problem. Show your work.

Mia brought grapes for snack.
She had 5 grapes.
Then she ate 1 of the grapes.

How many grapes did Mia have left?

NAME

DATE

Double Compare

Circle the pair of cards in each row that has more.

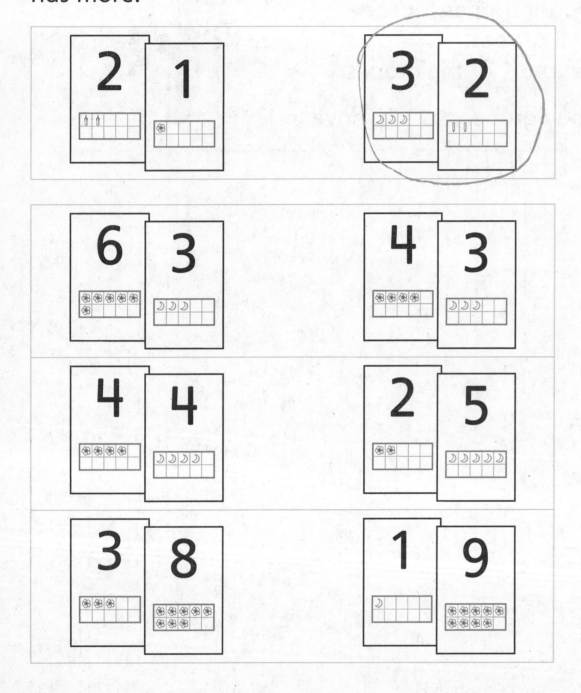

NOTE

Students combine two amounts and determine which total is greater.
MWI More

NAME

DATE

How Many Balls?

Solve the problem. Show your work.

Yoshio was cleaning up after recess.

He found 3 balls by the swings.
He found 2 balls by the slide.

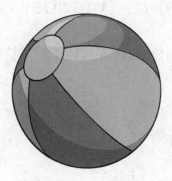

How many balls did Yoshio find?

Inventory Bag 2

Count the number of , , .

Count how many there are in all.

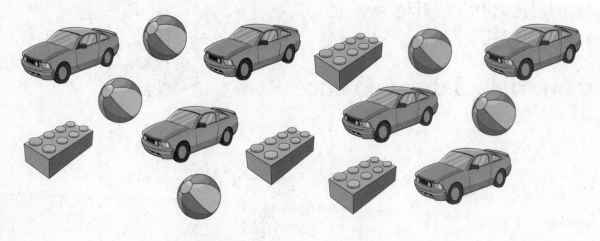

_____ cars

_____ balls

_____ blocks

How many are there in all? _____ toys

NOTE

Students practice counting and writing numbers.
MWI Ways to Count

UNIT 6 | 122 | SESSION 2.8   © SAVVAS Learning Company LLC.

NAME _____ DATE _____

Five Crayons in All

Solve the problem. Show your work.

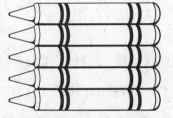

I have 5 crayons in all.

Some are red and some are blue.
How many of each color could I have?

How many blues? How many reds?

NAME   DATE

Double Compare at Home

Dear Family,

Tonight your child will teach you how to play the card game *Double Compare*. You will need the deck of Primary Number Cards that your child brought home earlier this year or you can use a regular deck of cards without the face cards.

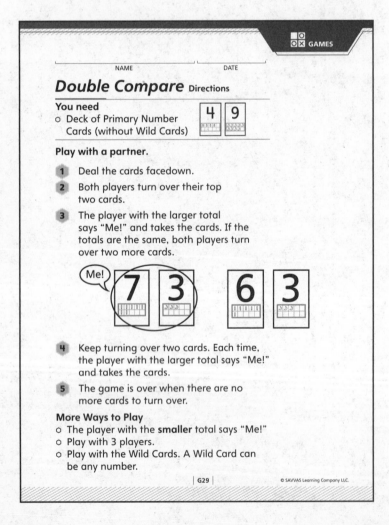

NOTE

Students combine amounts and determine which total is greater.
MWI **More**

NAME _____   DATE _____

Toss the Chips

Pretend you are playing *Toss the Chips* with 6 red and yellow chips. Fill in the chart for the yellow chips.

Red ●	Yellow ●	Total Number 6
2		
1		
4		
3		
5		
6		

NOTE

Students practice counting and breaking a number into two parts (6 = 2 + 4).
MWI **Ways to Make Six**

NAME _____ DATE _____

Six Crayons in All

Solve the problem. Show your work.

I have **6** crayons in all.

Some are red and some are blue.
How many of each color could I have?

How many blues? How many reds?

NAME

DATE

Make Six

In each row color the two cards that make 6.

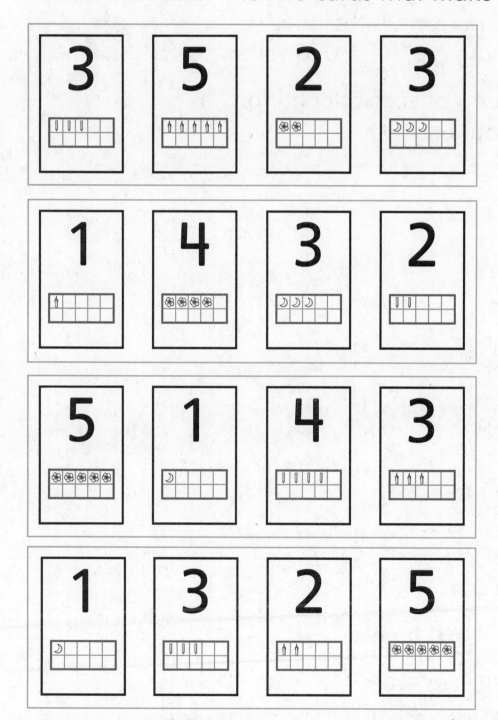

NOTE

Students practice counting and learning the combinations of two numbers that equal 6.
MWI Ways to Make Six

NAME   DATE

Inventory Bag: Buttons

Your inventory bag has buttons in it.
There are 15 buttons in the bag.
The buttons are red, blue, and yellow.

Show how many of each color button
could be in your bag.

NOTE

Students practice combining groups of objects that equal a specific number.
MWI A Story Problem About How Many of Each?

How Many Noses?
How Many Eyes?

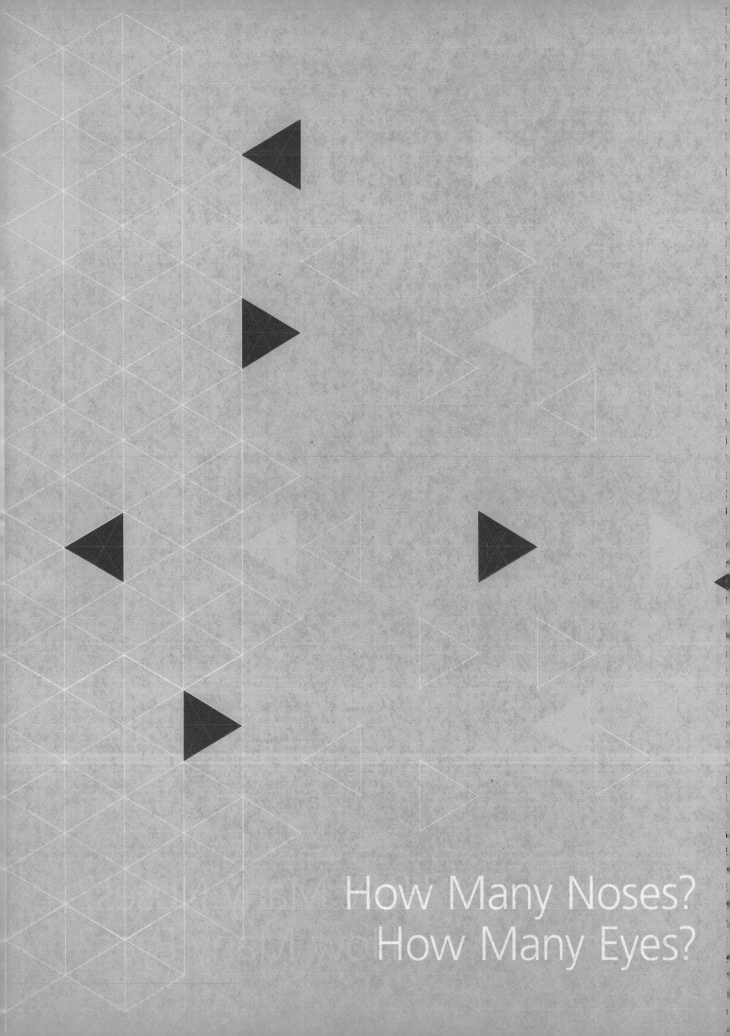

How Many Noses?
How Many Eyes?

About the Mathematics in This Unit

Dear Family,

Our class is starting a new unit in mathematics called *How Many Noses? How Many Eyes?* The focus of this unit is on identifying attributes of data and objects; collecting, sorting, and representing data; and using data to solve problems.

Throughout this unit, students will be working toward these goals:

Benchmarks/Goals	Examples
Sort a set of objects by a given attribute and order the groups based on the number in each	Grab a handful of pattern blocks. **1** How many of each block did you grab? <table><tr><td>Shape</td><td>⬡</td><td>▲</td><td>▱</td><td>■</td><td>▱</td><td>▲</td></tr><tr><td>How Many?</td><td>1</td><td>2</td><td>1</td><td>1</td><td>0</td><td>3</td></tr></table> **2** Put the numbers in order: 0 1 1 1 2 3
Using data to represent and solve a real-world problem	Are there enough chairs for everyone in our class? more chairs than kids

NAME   DATE

About the Mathematics in This Unit

In our math class, students engage in math problems and activities and discuss the underlying concepts. They are asked to share their reasoning and solutions. It is important that children solve math problems accurately in ways that make sense to them. At home, encourage your child to explain his or her math thinking to you.

In the coming weeks you will receive more information about this unit as well as suggestions for activities to do at home.

NAME _____ DATE _____

What's the Same?

Color the shapes that have 6 sides red.
Color the shapes that have 4 sides blue.

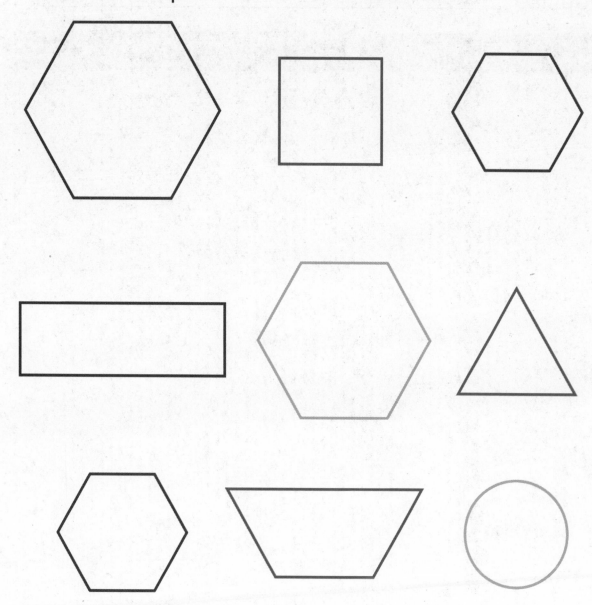

How many shapes have 6 sides? _____

How many shapes have 4 sides? _____

NOTE

Students practice identifying and sorting shapes based on the number of sides.
MWI Attributes of 2-D Shapes

UNIT 7 | 133 | SESSION 1.4   © SAVVAS Learning Company LLC.

NAME _____ DATE _____

"Do You Like . . . ?" Survey Chart

Do you like _____?

YES	NO

NAME

DATE

How Many Carrots?

Read the problem. Show your work.

Meg was making soup for dinner.

She bought 6 carrots.
She used 2 carrots.

How many carrots are left?

NOTE

Students practice solving subtraction story problems.
MWI **A Story Problem About Removing**

Related Activities to Try at Home

Dear Family,

The activities suggested below are related to the mathematics we are currently studying in school. Doing them with your child can enrich your child's mathematical learning.

Sorting Your child can sort collections of objects you have at home: coins, stamps, toys, containers, even laundry. He or she can sort just for fun or to organize some things in your home. As your child sorts a collection, ask him or her questions, such as: "How are some of the buttons the same? How could you sort them into groups? What is the same about all of these? Is there a different way you could sort them?" Your child can also count the number of items in each group and compare the totals.

Surveys In this unit, students conduct their own surveys. Help your child take a survey of your family, friends, or neighbors. Your child can choose a question that is of interest to him or her, create a sheet to record people's responses, ask people the question, and then record their responses. Afterward, ask your child some questions about the results of the survey. For example, ask: "What did you find out? How many people said they liked the ocean? How many people didn't like the ocean? Did more people like the ocean than did not? Were you surprised by people's responses?"

Counting to Collect Data You can encourage your child to collect data about the number of certain items in your home: How many forks are there? How many windows? How many chairs? How many doors?

© SAVVAS Learning Company LLC.

Related Activities to Try at Home

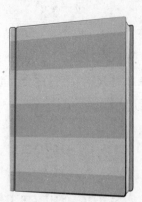

Math and Literature You can find the following books in your local library and read them together.

Aber, Linda Williams. *Grandma's Button Box (Math Matters)*.

Baer, Edith. *This Is the Way We Eat Our Lunch*.

Keenan, Sheila. *More or Less a Mess*.

Murphy, Stuart. *The Best Vacation Ever*.

Pluckrose, Henry Arthur. *Sorting (Math Counts)*.

Todd, Mark. *Food Trucks!*

NAME   DATE

How Many Pattern Blocks?

Mia grabbed two handfuls of blocks

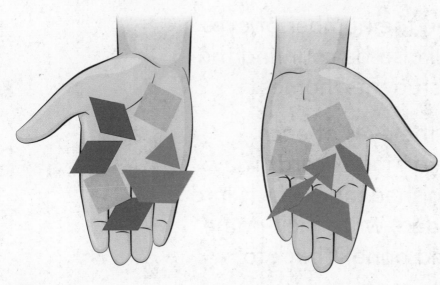

1 How many of each block did Mia grab?

Shape	⬡	▱	◆	◼	▱	▲
How Many?						

2 Put the numbers in order:

_____ _____ _____ _____ _____

3 How many did Mia grab in all? _____

NOTE

Students practice counting objects and writing numbers.
MWI Ordering Fewest to Most

NAME _____ DATE _____

Eyes at Home

Dear Family,

In class, we counted the number of eyes in our class. We will also be counting the number of eyes in students' homes.

Students will draw the eyes of each person at home on an index card. They should place the finished index cards into the envelope provided, write their name on the envelope and bring it back to school tomorrow.

If your child splits his or her time between different households, it's fine to include people from both homes.

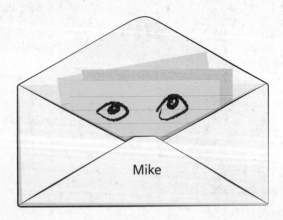

Mike

NOTE

Students practice counting by 2s.
MWI Counting by 2s

NAME   DATE

Do We Have Enough Chairs?: Collecting Chair Data

1 Keep track of the number of chairs you count here.

2 How many chairs are in our class? _____

3 When everyone is here, how many people are in our class? _____

4 Are there enough chairs for everyone in the class?

YES   NO

NAME

DATE

Eyes at Home

Choose an envelope. Count the number of people and the number of eyes. Record the data.

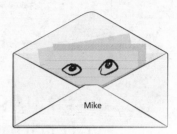

Mike

Name on Envelope	Number of People	Number of Eyes

NAME   DATE

How Many Eyes? How Many Noses?

There are 4 people.

How many noses are there? _____

How many eyes are there? _____

There are 7 people.

How many noses are there? _____

How many eyes are there? _____

NOTE

Students practice working with one-to-one and two-to-one relationships.
MWI **Ways to Count**

NAME _____ DATE _____

My Family: How Many Noses, Hands, and Fingers?

This is my family.

How many?

 Noses _____

 Hands _____

 ↑ Fingers _____

 → Legs _____

 Feet _____

 ↓ Toes _____

NOTE

Students practice counting body parts and writing numbers.
MWI **Ways to Count**

NAME _____ DATE _____

Favorite Meals

Beth asks her friends, "Which meal do you like best?" She marks their answers on the chart.

Breakfast	Lunch	Dinner

1 How many people like breakfast best? _____

2 Which meal do most people like best? _____

3 How many people did Beth ask? _____

4 Ask some friends which meal they like best. Record your data.

Breakfast	Lunch	Dinner

NOTE

Students analyze survey data and conduct a survey to collect data.
MWI **A Food Survey**

Ten Frames and Teen Numbers

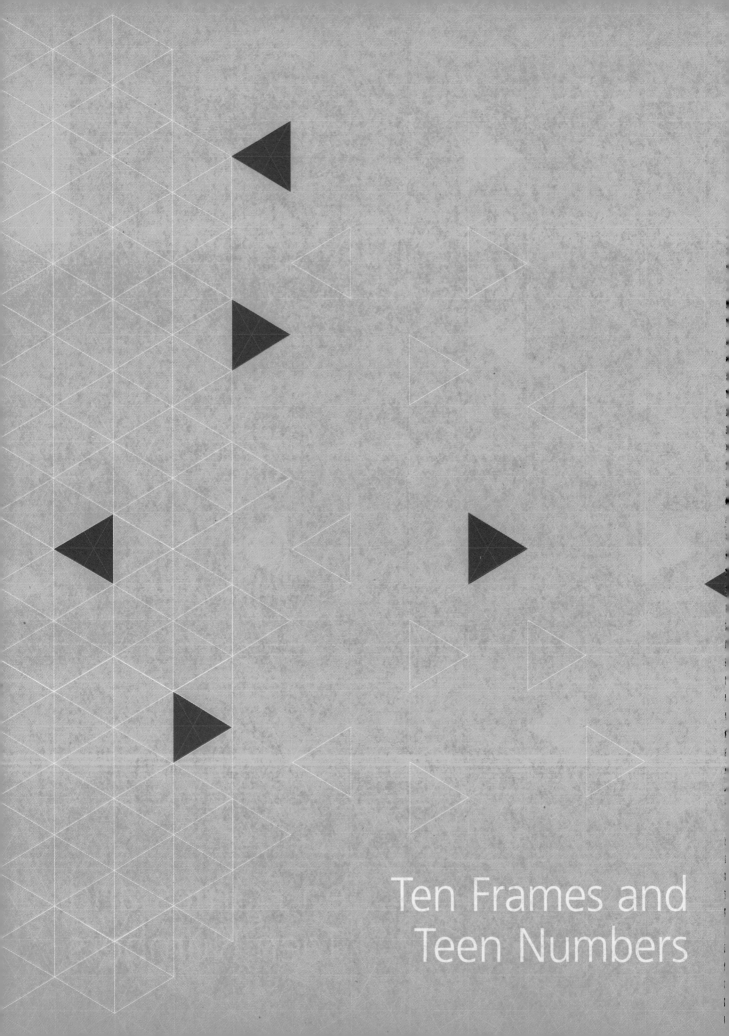

Ten Frames and
Teen Numbers

About the Mathematics in This Unit

Dear Family,

Our class is starting a new unit in mathematics called *Ten Frames and Teen Numbers*. The focus of this unit is on understanding and solving addition and subtraction problems in a variety of contexts (i.e., games, activities, story problems), recording and representing solutions on paper, making sense of the teen numbers (10–19) as a group of ten ones and some number of leftovers, and counting by 1s and 10s to 100.

Students solve story problems and discuss and compare their solution strategies with classmates. They practice counting by 10s as they count the number of fingers on 10 students. They play games where the cards that indicate how far to move (or how many to take) have "facts" on them, so that students develop fluency adding and subtracting within 5 (e.g., 3 + 2 and 4 − 1). They also work on a variety of activities that involve number combinations focusing specifically on combinations that make ten and on the teen numbers.

Throughout this unit, students will be working toward these goals:

Benchmarks/Goals	Examples
Represent and solve subtraction story problems within 10.	There are 6 birds in a tree. Two birds flew away. How many birds are left in the tree?
Count by 1s up to 100, starting from any number. Count by 10s to 100.	

© SAVVAS Learning Company LLC.

About the Mathematics in This Unit

Benchmarks/Goals	Examples
Add and subtract fluently within 5.	$2+3$ $5-1$
Given a number, figure out what number to add to make a total of 10.	$3 + \boxed{7} = 10$
Write the numbers to 20.	
Show that the teen numbers are made up of 10 ones and some leftover ones.	$10 + 3 = 13$

Write the numbers to 20 example:

		13							
		13							
		13				17			
	12	13		15		17			
10	12	13	14	15		17	18	19	
10	11	12	13	14	15	16	17	18	19
10+0	10+1	10+2	10+3	10+4	10+5	10+6	10+7	10+8	10+9

In our math class, students engage in math problems and activities and discuss the underlying concepts. They are asked to share their reasoning and solutions. It is important that children solve math problems accurately in ways that make sense to them. At home, encourage your child to explain his or her math thinking to you.

In the coming weeks, you will receive information about activities to do at home.

NAME   DATE

How Many Birds?

Solve the problem. Show your work.

There were 5 birds in a tree.
2 of the birds flew away.
How many birds are left in the tree?

How Many Pencils?

Solve the problem. Show your work.

There are 6 pencils in the box.
Max gave 3 pencils to Mia.
How many pencils are left in the box?

NAME   DATE

How Many Cars?

Solve the problem. Show your work.

Jack has 5 race cars.
He gave 3 of the cars to Max.
How many cars did Jack have left?

NOTE

Students practice solving a subtraction story problem.
MWI A Story Problem About Removing

NAME _____ DATE _____

Do You Like Pizza?

Max asked his friends if they liked pizza.
He showed the data on this chart.

Yes	No
✓ ✓ ✓ ✓ ✓ ✓ ✓ ✓ ✓ ✓ ✓ ✓	✓ ✓ ✓ ✓ ✓ ✓

1 How many people like pizza? _____

2 How many people do not like pizza? _____

3 How many people did Max ask? _____

4 Ask your family and friends if they like pizza.
Record your data on the chart below.

Yes	No

NOTE

Students analyze survey data and collect data from their family and friends.
MWI A Food Survey

NAME _____ DATE _____

How Many Ears? How Many Tails?

How many tails are there? _____

How many ears are there? _____

How many tails are there? _____

How many ears are there? _____

NOTE

Students practice working with one-to-one and one-to-two relationships.
MWI Ways to Count

NAME _____ DATE _____

Measuring Ourselves

Use cubes to measure parts of your body.
Record your measurements on the outline below.

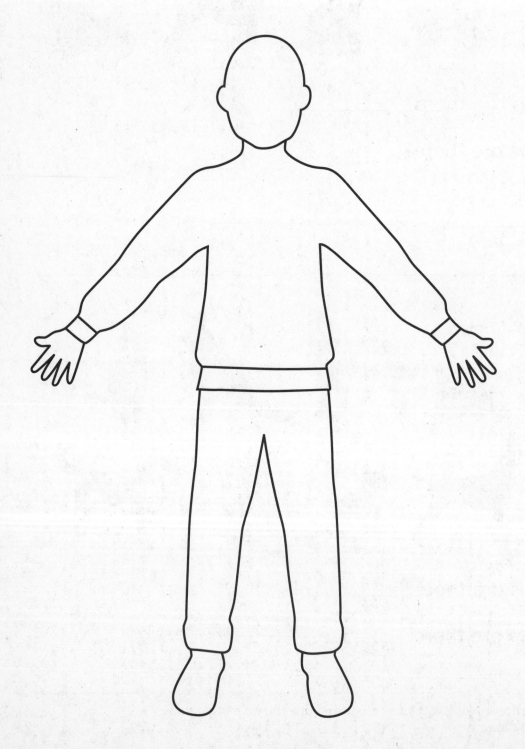

NAME

DATE

How Many to 10?

Fill in each Ten Frame to make 10. Write the equation.

Example:

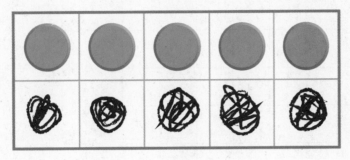

$$\underline{\quad 5 \quad} + \underline{\quad 5 \quad} = 10$$

1

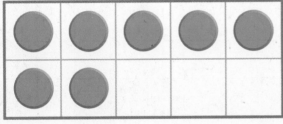

_____ + _____ = 10

2

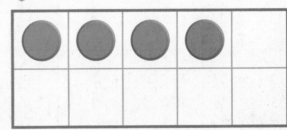

_____ + _____ = 10

3

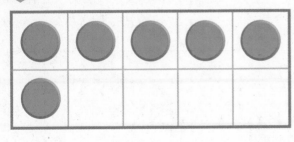

_____ + _____ = 10

4

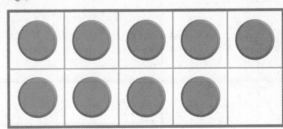

_____ + _____ = 10

Related Activities to Do at Home

Dear Family,

The activities suggested below are related to the mathematics we are currently studying in school. Doing them with your child can enrich your child's mathematical learning.

Counting While we continue to focus on strategies for counting a set of 20 objects accurately, we are also practicing the rote counting sequence with larger numbers. As a class, we often count aloud from one number to another. For example, we might start at 40 and count to 55. Find opportunities to count aloud together, letting your child pick the starting and ending numbers. In addition to counting by ones, we have begun to learn the counting by 10s sequence. You can also practice counting together by 10s to 100.

Addition and Subtraction We've been solving addition and subtraction problems, and thinking about strategies for solving subtraction problems. Find ways to present problems about common situations: "Usually, we have five people at our dinner table, but Maria is eating at a friend's house. How many people will there be?" Or, "There were six cookies, but Joe took two for snack. How many are left?" Encourage children to explain how they solve such problems. Most kindergarteners show the starting amount with counters or on their fingers, remove the amount that is taken away, and then count how many are left. Some may count back or "just know" some answers.

Combinations of 10 Ten is an important number in our number system, so we've been thinking about how to make 10. For example, how many dots are there? How many more do you need to have 10?

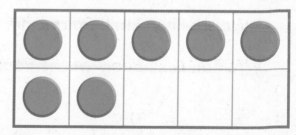

You can play a similar game with your fingers. Display a number of fingers, and ask, "How many to 10?" Students can represent and solve such problems on their fingers.

Related Activities to Do at Home

Measuring Weight We've been comparing objects to see which is heavier. Find opportunities to ask your child about the weight of different objects. For example, "What do you think is heavier, the milk carton or the cereal box? Why do you think so?" Encourage your child to hold one item in each hand to feel which weighs more.

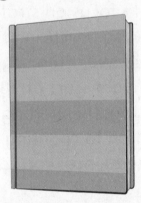

Math and Literature You can find these books in your local library and read them together. These books focus on *counting and measuring*:

Kroll, Virginia. *Equal Shmequal.*

Murphy, Stuart J. *Leaping Lizards.*

Sayre, April, and Sayre, Jeff. *One is a Snail, Ten is a Crab.*

Slater, Teddy. *98, 99, 100! Ready or Not, Here I Come!*

Viggers, Katie. *1 to 20, Animals Aplenty.*

Walsh, Ellen Stoll. *Balancing Act.*

Yektai, Niki. *Bears at the Beach Counting 10 to 20.*

NAME

DATE

Teen Number Hunt

Dear Family,

Your child is looking for examples of the numbers 10–19 around their home. They record the number they find and then draw a picture of where they found the number. For example, they might record the numbers 10, 11, and 12, and draw a picture of a clock and write the word "clock."

I found these teen numbers:	This is where I found them:

10   11   12   13   14   15   16   17   18   19

NOTE

Students look for and write examples of teen numbers.

MWI **Teen Numbers**

NAME

DATE

How Many Balls?

Solve the problem. Show your work.

Mia has 4 balls.
She gave 2 balls to Sam.
How many balls does Mia have left?

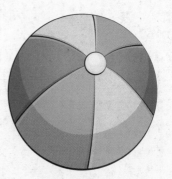

NOTE

Students practice solving a subtraction story problem.
MWI A Story Problem About Removing

NAME   DATE

Teens with Ten Frames

How many dots? Write the number.

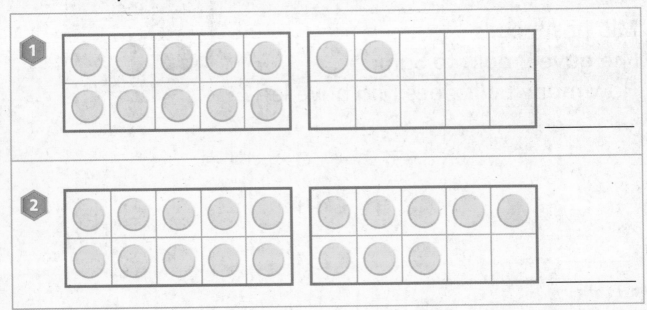

1. _____

2. _____

Fill in the empty Ten Frame to show the number.

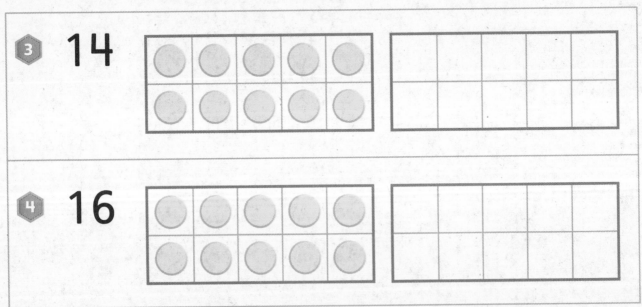

3. **14**

4. **16**

Comparing Weights

Draw the objects you weighed.
Circle the object that is heavier.

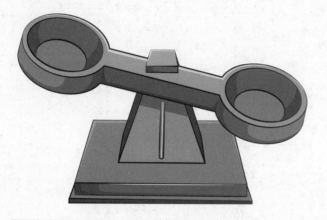

NAME _____ DATE _____

Measuring Weight with Cubes

Draw the object you weighed on one side.
Draw the cubes on the other side.

We measured with this: .

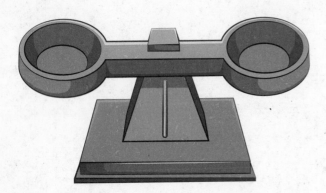

It weighs _____ cubes.

It weighs _____ cubes.

NAME   DATE

Measuring Weight with Pennies

Draw the object you weighed on one side.
Draw the pennies on the other side.

We measured with this: .

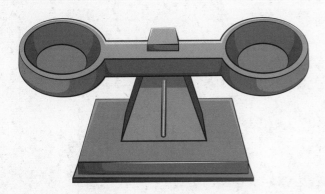

It weighs _____ pennies.

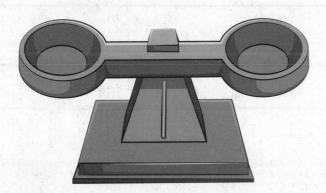

It weighs _____ pennies.

© SAVVAS Learning Company LLC.

NAME

DATE

How Many Strawberries?

Solve the problem. Show your work.

Meg had 5 strawberries in her lunch box.
She ate 4 of them for a snack.
How many did she have left?

NAME _____ DATE _____

Teens with Ten Frames 2

How many dots? Write the number.

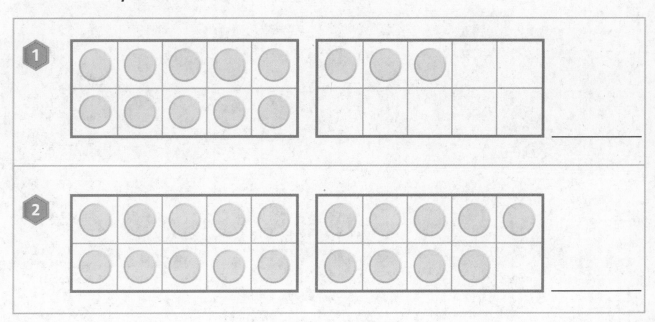

1 _____

2 _____

Fill in the empty Ten Frame to show the number.

3 **20**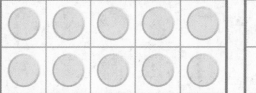

4 **15**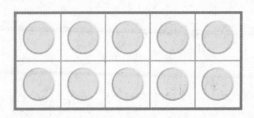

NOTA

Students represent a quantity with numbers and on Ten Frames.
MWI **Ten Frames**